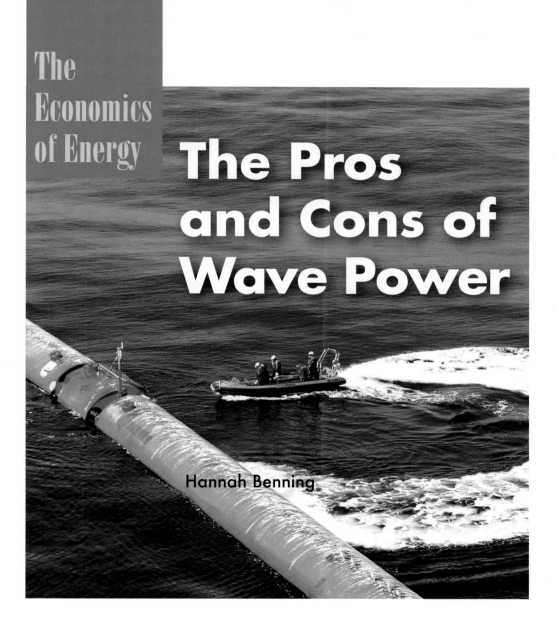

The Economics
of Energy

The Pros and Cons of Wave Power

Hannah Benning

Cavendish
Square

New York

Published in 2016 by Cavendish Square Publishing, LLC
243 5th Avenue, Suite 136, New York, NY 10016

Copyright © 2016 by Cavendish Square Publishing, LLC

First Edition

Website: cavendishsq.com

This publication represents the opinions and views of the author based on his or her personal experience, knowledge, and research. The information in this book serves as a general guide only. The author and publisher have used their best efforts in preparing this book and disclaim liability rising directly or indirectly from the use and application of this book.

CPSIA Compliance Information: Batch #CW16CSQ

All websites were available and accurate when this book was sent to press.

Library of Congress Cataloging-in-Publication Data

Benning, Hannah, author.
The pros and cons of wave power / Hannah Benning.
pages cm. — (The economics of energy)
Includes index.
ISBN 978-1-5026-0958-8 (hardcover) ISBN 978-1-5026-0959-5 (ebook)
1. Ocean wave power. 2. Water-power. 3. Electric utilities—United States. I. Title.
TC147.B475 2016
333.91'4—dc23
2015036265

Editorial Director: David McNamara
Editor: Amy Hayes/Ryan Nagelhout
Copy Editor: Nathan Heidelberger
Art Director: Jeffrey Talbot

Designer: Amy Greenan
Production Manager: Jennifer Ryder-Talbot
Production Editor: Renni Johnson
Photo Researcher: J8 Media

Printed in the United States of America

Table of Contents

This Pelamis machine is one of three working off the coast of Portugal.

Chapter 1

Uncharted Waters

Harnessing energy from waves has been studied for some time. Tests of wave devices date back to the early twentieth century. Despite its early roots, however, testing individual models best represents the majority of wave energy activity today. There are fewer large-scale **wave farms,** or a series of wave energy devices together producing electricity, and more individual wave energy devices in the testing phases. Wave energy has not become a popular source of energy.

What is holding up wave energy? Wave energy devices are being tested. However, unlike wind or solar power, wave energy still has a variety of models that are trying to harness it. The perfect model for the waves just hasn't been discovered. There isn't one model exclusively holding all the answers. Also, wave energy research needs funding. It can be difficult to find funding for tests when your device isn't producing electricity at a significant scale quite yet and many risks are still involved.

Yet, the market is shifting, resulting in more funding, larger projects, and testing sites. Understanding the diversity of the wave energy approaches and models is important when forming a complete picture of wave energy's pros and cons. The variety of wave energy models makes for quite an exciting picture. There are seabed devices, buoy or floating devices, and shoreline and offshore devices, not to mention tidal wave power.

Within each of these categories, there are even more device models competing for the wave energy market. With a diverse pool of technologies comes a diverse set of problems and solutions. Considering the specific details of each kind of device will help us gain a clearer picture of the benefits of wave energy and the obstacles to its widespread adoption.

One of the most credible problems wave energy faces is also the most ironic: the great yet destructive power of waves. This power is the source of wave energy electricity and it offers the opportunity to generate electricity with zero **carbon emissions**. However, it is maintained that wave power can be destructive, which is a major threat to wave energy devices. They must be durable. People who depend on wave energy cannot afford for devices to be destroyed by a storm.

Measuring Energy Consumption

As wave energy technology improves, the amount of electricity it will be able to produce will increase. In order to fully appreciate these improvements, it is important to understand how many homes and cities these wave energy devices can actually support.

Energy is needed to power homes, suburbs, and cities. A typical household needs roughly 1 **kilowatt (kW)** to power it. A kilowatt is a unit of power. If you have a 60-**watt (W)** light bulb (watts are a smaller unit of power; there are 1,000 watts in every kilowatt), when the light is turned on, that light bulb uses 60 watts of **instantaneous power**, or power being consumed right now. So if a household needs about 1 kilowatt to power it, that means in order to light your home, heat or cool it, power your refrigerator, and use your appliances (such as a laptop), on average you will need at least 1 kilowatt of instantaneous power.

Of course, if you turn off all your lights and air conditioning in the summer, you would be using less power. A **kilowatt-hour (kWh)** is a unit used to measure energy. It represents how much power a person or household consumes on average within an hour. Depending on the time period you are measuring, the kilowatt-hours figure will differ. For example, the amount of kilowatt-hours you use for a year will differ from the amount you use for a weekend. The weekend amount will be much less. In 2013, the US Energy Information Administration reported that an average American household used 10,908 kWh per year, or an average of 909 kWh per month.

It is important to understand the difference between the kilowatt and the kilowatt-hour and why we need to measure both. For example, if you go on vacation, the number of kilowatt-hours used in your house for the week you are gone will be far less than the number of kilowatt-hours needed for when you are home. Why? Because when you are on vacation, you are not turning on lights, running the dishwasher, or using any other appliances. However, whether you are home or away, the number of kilowatts needed to power your home stays the same. For example, if you have a 60-watt light bulb, the light needs 60 watts to work. It might not be using any energy when it is off, but 60 watts of power are what is needed for it to light the room. Therefore, a kilowatt is a unit of power, while a kilowatt-hour measures power consumed or produced by the hour over a period of time—a day, a month, a year, or more.

A DEEPER DIVE

From Wind to Wave

Far out at sea a storm emerges. From the chaotic weather, tall, strong waves are born and travel great distances. What causes these chaotic storms? From where does the massive amount of energy the ocean carries originate?

Strong waves are formed by **low-pressure systems,** or warm wind. As the wind blows across the water's surface, some of the wind's kinetic energy is transferred to the water, forming waves. These waves travel long distances without losing significant energy, making them reliable sources of renewable energy.

The low-pressure systems that create waves are formed by solar energy from the sun. The sun heats the planet at differing temperatures. These unequal temperatures create low-pressure systems and **high-pressure systems.** A high-pressure system is made up of cool air and forms fair weather. The low-pressure systems that form ocean storms create strong waves that travel for miles to our coastlines.

Waves from ocean storms can travel long distances without losing energy, making the ocean an optimal energy source.

Imagine your home, all your appliances, the light from your lamps, and the heat from your stove powered without any carbon emissions. Imagine your city powered by the same waves you surf on, or that nip at your toes on a beach. This is the possibility that the ocean presents us. Researchers, engineers, and entrepreneurs are working hard to make this possibility a reality.

When we think about electricity, we often picture light bulbs, but there are many different appliances in your home powered by electricity.

A good way to find out how much electricity your house uses is to take a look at your electricity bill, which is usually measured in kilowatt-hours. However, there are other ways for you to learn the exact amount of kilowatts your home requires. Take a look at some of your appliances around the house. The wattage needed to power your devices is usually stamped somewhere on them. For example, you might have a 1.1-kilowatt microwave (or 1,100 watts). A clock radio might need 10 watts. An LED light bulb often needs 10 watts, too.

Some appliances will record energy consumption in volts (V) and amps (A) instead of watts. Watts are the amount of power consumed or generated, while volts measure the pressure or force of energy. The volts (V)

Waves can help turn the lights on in your home, but you can also help conserve energy by being conscientious of the way you use electricity.

A Timeline of Wave Power

1909 Alva A. Reynolds invents a shoreline wave power device that lights lamps along California's Huntington Beach Wharf

1985 Norway builds a tapered channel system (TAPCHAN)

1988 Norway's TAPCHAN is destroyed by strong storm waves

1997 Testing begins on Ocean Power Technologies' (OPT) PowerBuoy floating device design

2000 LIMPET, an oscillating water column, is installed in Islay, Scotland

2004 Pelamis Wave Power tests their first full-scale prototype

2007 Finavera's AquaBuOY sinks during its testing phase, demonstrating the initial costliness and risk necessary when testing novel renewable energies

2008 Scottish government announces the Saltire Prize, a £10 million prize for the winning marine energy design, allowing organizations to test new designs over an extensive period of time

2009 Pelamis Wave Power's P2 is the first wave energy device purchased by a utility company

2011 Electric Power Research Institute (EPRI) reports the United States can provide 1,170 terawatt-hours yearly in wave energy

2014 US Navy and US Department of Energy partner to test three wave energy devices at Hawaii's energy test site, connecting devices to the Hawaiian grid; M3 Wave completes its first successful deployment of a DMP floor bed device, the first of its kind

2015 Wave Energy Scotland (WES) provides funding for innovative marine energy project testing; Chile partners with France's naval defense and marine energy organization, DCSN, to build a marine energy research and development center in South America; it is announced that Columbia Power Technologies' StingRAY will be tested in Oahu, Hawaii, for twelve months in 2016 with funding provided by the Naval Facilities and Engineering Command

multiplied by amps (A), the current or amount of electricity used, will equal the number of watts. There are converters online that will translate volts and amps into watts. You can look them up if you want to know how much electricity certain appliances that only give the volts and amps need.

Understanding electricity consumption helps us become responsible energy users and helps us understand the accomplishments wave energy devices make. With each new model, the number of kilowatts of power produced increases. Understanding the relationship between electricity consumed and produced will be relevant when looking at these progresses. With improvements and the implementation of new wave farms, wave energy can positively impact our environment and economy by offering carbon-free energy.

Unpredictable Waters

Early investigations of wave energy were filled with discoveries and obstacles. The first tests revealed the great contradiction of wave energy. The energy of powerful waves that makes them important to harness also destroys the devices used to harness the energy. Alva A. Reynolds discovered the irony of this great power.

On December 19, 1909, the *Los Angeles Herald* reported the inventor's extraordinary invention. Reynolds invented a device that utilized the power of waves. The device was installed on the Huntington Beach Wharf in California and was used to light lamps along the beach. Reynolds was praised for his breakthrough in harnessing wave power.

Reynolds was truly ahead of his time. Unfortunately, his shoreline device was eventually claimed by a storm. Reynolds's experiment was

The consistent power of waves is both valuable and frightening. Too much power in waves can cause lots of damage.

one of many to follow. However, the fear that important devices may be destroyed by the waves they try to harness still plagues many wave energy investors today. Millions of dollars are put into the development of model devices for testing. The risks and costs of failure make it clear that it is important to test devices, even though testing itself can be costly.

Different Approaches to Wave Energy

Although Reynolds created a shoreline device that captured the energy of the waves in the early 1900s, harnessing wave energy is a rather contemporary breakthrough in renewable energy. In other words, much of the development in wave energy began in the second half of the twentieth century and continues to advance today. The push for renewable and sustainable energy sources could be one reason for this shift in interest toward the mysterious power of the sea.

Much of the progress of wave energy is shown by the many trials and errors in testing new devices. Over time, this dedication has created increased interest in wave energy through the development of contests, funding, and new partnerships to support wave technology. Commercialization of wave energy farms, which is the goal of these wave energy companies, is in sight.

Fixed Devices

There are many models of wave energy devices that use different techniques to capture the energy of waves. All of them transfer the motion of water into electricity, usually through a **generator** of some sort.

While there are many different companies creating wave power machines, most devices fall into one of only a few design categories.

Three main methods are TAPCHAN systems, oscillating water column (OWC) devices, and floating or buoy systems. However, there are many departures from these models, such as M3 Wave's ocean floor device. Devices are located on the shore, such as oscillating water columns and TAPCHAN systems, or out at sea, such as the floating devices.

TAPCHANs: Tapered Channel Systems

A TAPCHAN is a tapered channel system, and it generates energy. To illustrate a TAPCHAN system's individual benefits and pitfalls, it's important to understand the structure and how it functions.

TAPCHAN systems are giant concrete reservoirs, like artificial lakes. A TAPCHAN system is built into a coastal cliff so that it rests above sea level. As waves crash into the cliffside, the TAPCHAN fills with water. How are the waves able to fill the reservoir if it's above sea level? This is where the tapered channel comes into play. The tapered channel leads up to the reservoir opening. As the waves fill the channel, it narrows, increasing the height of the waves until they spill into the reservoir. The water that is collected in the reservoir is then fed back into the ocean through a tube. In this tube is a Kaplan turbine. As the water channels into this tube, it moves the Kaplan turbine and this movement is converted into electricity. The tube travels down and opens up below sea level back into the ocean.

A TAPCHAN is similar to a dam in the way that it stores water and then uses the water's potential energy. However, TAPCHAN systems don't carry the negative environmental alterations that hydropower dams do. Where dams alter the shape of rivers, create lakes, and affect ecosystems, TAPCHAN systems do not. TAPCHAN systems, in contrast, are like giant, rectangular, concrete buckets of water on coastal cliffs.

Because TAPCHAN systems can store water, they can provide energy even when there aren't strong waves. It is important for the future of wave energy development that a TAPCHAN system can provide electricity even when wave conditions aren't ideal. The ability to use stored potential energy makes TAPCHAN systems a reliable source of energy. Oscillating water columns (OWCs) and floating devices face challenges because they depend on the constant movement of waves to produce energy.

TAPCHAN systems require deep waters and a location that allows the device to rest above sea level. These limitations can make TAPCHAN systems impractical because not all areas that need energy have these conditions. Floating devices, on the other hand, do not need these same conditions to function. Additionally, OWCs also do not share the same geographical limitations as TAPCHANs, making geographical restriction of this kind a disadvantage that other wave energy technologies do not share.

The OWC: Oscillating Water Column

The OWC is another major shoreline device. It looks like an oversized storm drain. The design of an OWC appears simple: it is visually unobtrusive and constructed out of concrete. Unlike a TAPCHAN, this kind of wave power plant needs constant waves to produce electricity. It does not store water. In fact, the OWC's turbine does not come in contact with water. How can the turbine move if it does not come in contact with the waves?

OWCs use a Wells turbine, whose unique design allows the turbine blades to turn no matter which way the air moves. There is an air opening at the top of the OWC and another opening submerged in the water where waves come in. The turbine is located near the top opening, where air can be pushed out of the OWC by the force of the waves. Waves come

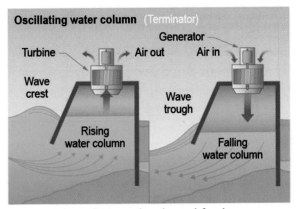

Oscillating water column (Terminator)

Generator

Turbine — Air out

Air in

Wave crest

Wave trough

Rising water column

Falling water column

An OWC pushes air back and forth through its Wells turbine using the force of waves. The movement of the turbine is then converted into electricity.

into the OWC, forcing air up and out, turning the turbine. As the waves retreat, air is also sucked back into the OWC, continuing to move the turbine. The Wells turbine allows the OWC to generate consistent energy regardless of the direction of airflow. The energy from this turbine is thenconverted into electricity.

Similar to the TAPCHAN, an OWC's shoreline location and concrete structure protect it from being destroyed or consumed by storm waves. However, the OWC does not have an accessible reservoir of potential energy. OWCs rely entirely on the constant crashing of waves on the shoreline. Luckily, waves are consistent—they happen every day. Because of the reliability of the waves, the OWC can consistently produce electricity. However, the amount of electricity produced changes according to the size and force of the waves.

Fixed shoreline devices are durable, safe, and low risk. Why not make a fixed device offshore? One that doesn't need certain shoreline conditions to produce energy and can capture kinetic energy from the waves out at sea? Two engineers have done just this. There is a new, third fixed device. The Delos-Reyes Morrow Pressure Device (DMP) captures wave power from a fixed position on the seabed off the coast. This device presents many solutions to the problems created by floating buoy devices.

Wave Energy that Floats

The number of different floating devices is extraordinary in this growing market. While there are only a few different types of shoreline devices, there are a variety of different floating devices, also known as buoys. Each device has a specific history and company that helped create it. Due to the need for testing, power companies enter partnerships with educational institutes and government organizations to help get devices out of the planning stages and into the water.

Pelamis Wave Converter

Floating devices are at high risk for being destroyed. Ocean storms and strong currents can break apart these devices, which are put directly into the ocean. However, companies work hard to design floating devices that can withstand the variability and power of ocean waves. Their long-term testing has proven successful.

One company known for their floating devices was Pelamis. It developed a device resembling a giant snake that floated on the water, shifting back and forth as the waves passed under it. Called the Pelamis Wave Energy Converter, it was made up of a series of connected, large, tube-like parts. The joints, or hinges, contained **hydraulic rams**, or pumps. In the ocean, the waves caused the hydraulic rams to move. The pumps opened and closed as the water passed through them. As the water of the ocean moved back and forth, the Pelamis Wave Energy Converter moved with the waves and caused the hinges to shift. Imagine an oiled rod moving forward and backward through a cylinder-like structure. The kinetic energy from this movement of the pumps is

Pelamis Wave Power devices were designed and strategically tested to withstand the ocean's force, but ocean waters can often be unpredictable.

converted into electricity in an electric generator and then is transferred to shore by a cable.

In Great Britain in 2004, a Pelamis prototype became the first offshore wave energy device to feed energy into a **national grid**, or the network of high-voltage power lines connecting a country's major power stations. According to the company's calculated testing strategy, each converter was tested first at a variety of wave heights and intensities. This allowed the company to identify risks, manage them, and improve the models. One such model was the P2 Pelamis Wave Energy Converter, first tested in 2010 and designed to have a power capacity of up to 750 kilowatts. Unfortunately, the Pelamis company went out of business in 2014 after failing to secure funding for developing technologies.

PowerBuoy

Ocean Power Technologies (OPT) was founded in 1994 in the United States with a vision to utilize the ocean's energy in a unique way. The company worked to design the PowerBuoy.

The PowerBuoy resembles a normal buoy that would point out a rock or an anchor. It includes a yellow float that sits on top of the water. However, under the water it has a spar, or a long black tube; a heave plate, which is situated at the bottom of the device but floating above the seafloor; cables; and an undersea substation situated on the ocean floor. As the float moves back and forth with the waves, a mechanical system in the spar converts the linear motion of the float into a rotary movement that is used to drive generators. These generators then produce electricity. Because of this design, the PowerBuoy is able to generate electricity even in mild wave conditions.

A single PowerBuoy can harness power ranging from 350 watts to 15 kilowatts as described by OPT. If an average household uses 1 kW, one PowerBuoy could potentially power fifteen households. Like the TAPCHAN system, the PowerBouy can provide continuous power in any weather. The PowerBouy is even able to store power during mild wave conditions if necessary. It is the first floating device able to conserve power and provides new possibilities that previously were only available to shoreline devices.

Having undergone testing since 1997, the PowerBuoy is appealing to potential investors. Longer testing periods allow for improvements to be made, which minimizes risk. This extensive testing period also proves that the PowerBuoy can reliably produce electricity.

StingRAY

The StingRAY is a bright beacon for wave energy. Columbia Power Technologies, formed in 2005, designed this device after researching, testing, and modifying previous designs. The creators found ways to optimize the design's ability to harness wave power. As reported by Elizabeth Rusch in *The Next Wave*, the StingRAY can generate 330 kW of electricity, enough to potentially power 330 homes.

The StingRAY has a multiple float system that makes it unique. Columbia Power Technologies designed the device so that each float has its own **drive shaft**—a rotating shaft that transmits power—connected to a rotary generator. Within the floats are spars that independently react to ocean waves. Each float functions on its own—rather than together—in response to the oncoming waves, offering the StingRAY a great deal of free movement. The multiple floats system was designed so that the

A unique feature of the PowerBuoy is its ability to harness electricity even in mild wave conditions.

The StingRAY's multiple buoy system allows it to move with the waves, making it a good match for lively waters.

StingRAY can withstand high ocean waves and protect itself. The system helps the StingRAY move with the waves while also efficiently securing wave energy for electricity.

In addition to the PowerBuoy and Pelamis wave converter, the StingRAY design has established a promising solution to wave power's biggest question: How will these floating devices survive major waves? StingRAY answers this with its ability to still reliably produce electricity in violent weather conditions. StingRAY's unique multiple float feature demonstrates that buoy devices can work with the waves. Columbia Power's simple design has already gained support by the US Navy, which has contracted Columbia Power to deploy StingRAY at its Wave Energy Test Site in Oahu, Hawaii.

TAPCHAN and OWC systems don't have the same problems as floating devices. Due to the fact that their shoreline location provides added protection, they don't carry the same threat of demolition. A large concrete reservoir, in the case of TAPCHAN, or a concrete, storm drain–like structure, in the case of OWC, promises durability in the face of ocean storms. Lower risk is always more appealing when it comes to product investment, and it can speed up improvement and commercial manufacturing. In this way, it has been easier for shoreline devices to progress from testing to manufacturing stages than for floating devices.

However, buoy systems have shown a lot of promise. The few buoy designs explored here are only a sample of the many other designs present today. Representative of some unique approaches to wave energy, the information gathered from these examples may form a basis for further understanding of buoy devices. And who knows? There may be more unique approaches on the horizon.

It Doesn't Need to Float

Mike Morrow, Mike Delos-Reyes, and Mike Miller formed a company called M3 Wave to develop and test a wave energy device Delos-Reyes and Morrow originally designed when they were in college. Delos-Reyes and Morrow wondered why no one had created an offshore device that sat securely on the ocean floor. They felt this would solve some of the many problems of floating devices. For instance, concerns had been raised about how floating devices might affect local habitats and wildlife, fishing industries, and coastal tourism. A seabed device may not create as many disruptions.

The Delos-Reyes Morrow Pressure Device (DMP) uses the force of passing waves to push air through a tube that houses a turbine. This concept of using waves to push air is somewhat similar to the oscillating water column. However, unlike the OWC, the DMP uses the wave pressure to impact air trapped in an enclosed bag.

Resting on the ocean floor close to the coast, the DMP consists of two main parts: two air chambers and a long tube that contains a bidirectional turbine. As a wave passes over the first chamber, chamber A, air is forced through the tube and the bidirectional turbine, causing the turbine to spin. Then air pressure increases in the second chamber, chamber B. As the same wave passes over chamber B, the pressure from the wave then pushes the air back through the tube into chamber A. The motion of the bidirectional turbine is converted to electricity by an electrical generator that is then transferred to shore by cables.

The DMP has many attractive qualities. For one thing, there are no exposed parts so it does not obstruct its surrounding environment. It

Like the StingRAY, the DMP presents a solution to the destructive forces of big waves. Unlike the StingRAY, however, the DMP's solution is to rest below the surface.

does not disrupt fishing industries and, with minimal visibility, it will not impact coastal tourism. Resting on the ocean floor, it is unlikely to relocate local wildlife. However, there are concerns about seafloor devices creating artificial reefs. Artificial reefs can complement local habitats or attract invasive species. The only way to determine the exact impact is to deploy the devices and monitor them. Despite these fears, many believe it is unlikely to disrupt the habitat that it will be placed in.

The DMP has the potential to solve many wave energy problems. Unlike the StingRAY, the DMP does not need complex floating devices, which could curb costs. M3 Wave completed its first successful deployment of the device off the coast of Oregon in 2014, a marker for future success.

Bigger Waters

Engineers, researchers, government officials, and educators are working out the particulars of wave energy. While they try to come up with the most efficient and durable model, the market slowly moves from testing phases to commercialized phases where production can occur at a larger scale. Many feel the promise of wave energy and a carbon-free footprint will be realized with testing, time, and opportunity.

CRITICAL THINKING

- What advantages and disadvantages might result from so many differing wave energy devices?

- Based on the information you have learned in this chapter, which device would you choose to harness wave energy? What successes and failures do you anticipate?

- What problems do you think M3 Wave's DMP device solves for wave energy?

- What challenges might have prevented wave energy from becoming quickly commercialized?

- It has been claimed that wave energy is more reliable than wind or solar energy. Why do you think this might be?

- Based on the appliances you use, what are some ways you could use less electricity in a given day?

Moving the energy created by wave power and connecting wave energy machines to the grid is one problem engineers face in working with this renewable energy source.

Chapter 2

Advantages of Wave Power

Wave energy has a lot of advantages even over other renewable resources. The electricity provided by waves is more dependable than wind and solar sources, and wave energy has the potential to be less harmful than wind.

Wave energy is capable of powering entire towns. It is also more convenient than you may expect: about 44 percent of the world's population lives within 93 miles (150 kilometers) of the coast, where waves are and where wave power would be most effective. Although wave energy faces difficulties in developing the best model to harness the waves, with significant steps wave energy can provide carbon-free energy to many people.

The Wave That Returns

One of the biggest advantages to waves is that they're always rolling and crashing. Powerful waves originate from storms out at sea. These storm waves travel long distances without significant energy loss. An abundance of potential energy is housed in each wave. This feature makes wave

A DEEPER DIVE

The Small Wave

As reported by the Ocean Energy Council located in West Palm Beach, Florida, a wave contains about one thousand times the kinetic energy of wind. Also, the amount of energy produced by wind varies by the time of day. Wind **velocity** dies down in the nighttime and morning hours. Another reason why wave energy is superior to wind energy is that a wave can produce the same amount of energy as wind in a fraction of the space. A big drawback of some renewable energy sources is the amount of space they take up. Wave energy does not have this problem. Devices can be installed in less space with little visibility. The Ocean Energy Council reports that wave energy takes up less area than wind and requires no roads to access it, which lowers the costs for constructing and deploying devices. Low visibility complements wave energy's efficient output: more power from a smaller device and area is a definite plus.

What about solar power? How do waves compare to this renewable energy resource? Solar power is only available during the daytime. As a result, solar power can only produce electricity during a limited time. Waves, in comparison, do not quit. Wave power exists around the clock.

Waves don't lose significant amounts of energy as they travel to shore.

energy reliable. Reliability makes wave energy a secure new renewable energy source to invest in and a real option that could power the future.

Friends of the Waves

People are concerned that wave energy might have a negative effect on local wildlife and their habitats. However, there is no conclusive evidence thus far. Some studies have attempted to address problems possibly

Considering the safety and impact on marine wildlife is imperative when developing new wave energy sources.

created by wave energy devices, including artificial reefs and habitat disruption. The results have been positive.

For example, researchers wanted to find out how dangerous turbine blades are. Fish biologist Gayle Zydlewski studied fish responses to Ocean Renewable Power's tidal unit based in Maine. Zydlewski asserted that based on her studies, fish avoided the unit. This observation is a good sign for marine energy advocates and local habitat preservationists. Keep in mind, however, that Zydlewski only studied one tidal unit. Therefore, scientists do not know what would happen when more than one unit is in one area. However, just in case, the US Department of Energy hired biologists to actually test how fish respond to being sent through the turbines and reported that there was no permanent damage.

Puget Sound, which is outside of Seattle, Washington, serves as a home to the endangered orca, also known as the killer whale. With the anticipation of housing **tidal turbines**, the US Department of Energy asked researchers to conduct tests on how these turbines could affect orcas. The worst-case scenario was the possibility of an orca putting his or her head in one of the turbines. They concluded with some certainty that there would be no permanent damage and that the blade would only leave a bruise. The studies conducted in 2012 and 2013 were positive but not definitive, meaning more studies need to be done in order to know for sure if orcas will be harmed.

Seabed Safety

Many people believe the Delos-Reyes Morrow Pressure device would have minimal impact on the environment and would last longer than other devices. M3 Wave's DMP device sits on the ocean floor, which protects it from destructive waves and is largely unobtrusive. Surfers and coastal markets such as tourism would not have to worry about the impact of such a device because the DMP is ultimately invisible from the surface. Fishing and shipping markets would remain unaffected as well. The DMP is not a hazard for ships navigating waters because it is not a surface obstruction. Fish and other marine animals also will not be troubled with navigating around the device. Finally, the lack of exposed parts provides safety to marine wildlife as well. DMP's location and design offer solutions to so many problems and broaden the availability of locations for wave energy.

The Beast in the Storm

Giant storm waves have presented concerns for our floating wave energy devices, and engineers have gone to work. The StingRAY, developed by Columbia Power, is one such device created to work with these monster waves. Built with multiple floats, the device has been tested against 26-foot (8-meter) and 47-foot (14 m) waves. StingRAY survived these tests by using its safer survival mode, and its power generation was impressive: 330 kW on average and up to 500 kW during larger, storm-like waves. The largest recorded storm wave was at a height of 95 feet (29 m). StingRAY is a potential challenger for these giant beasts.

Predictable and Quiet

Wind produces waves that can retain their energy over long distances. They are a consistent source of energy. Wave energy is predictable and

Wave energy devices are constantly battling the harsh ocean conditions, often made worse by large storms.

therefore reliable. As mentioned before, the fact that waves travel long distances without significant energy loss adds to this reliability.

Although there are arguments against wave energy that claim the buoys' visibility is obtrusive, there are advantages to its visibility.

Visibility helps notify ships of the buoys' presence, which in turn prevents accidents and unneeded costs. In comparison with other renewable energy sources, wave energy devices are much quieter and less obtrusive than wind energy devices, which can be over 300 feet (91 m) tall.

Partnership Possibilities

Growing partnerships with the US Navy and various educational institutions have given wave energy developers opportunities to test devices at low costs. Expenses for facilities can be high and finding partners such as the US Navy to fund experimental projects greatly speeds up this process. Dr. Annette von Jouanne of Oregon State University helped found the Northwest National Marine Renewable Energy Center (NNMREC), which gives many companies the opportunity to test projects for a small fee. Governmental and educational partnerships are growing and they enable wave energy to grow as well.

Artificial Reefs

Like piers and other man-made structures, ocean energy devices may provide a place for the growth of artificial reefs. These reefs can enhance biodiversity and replenish areas in need. The reefs can either be protected, giving endangered species a safe space to live, or used to increase production for local fishing markets. Depending on the intended use, there can be environmental or economic benefits. For example, artificial reefs can be used for tourism, allowing tourists to dive and view the reefs. Reefs can also be studied by experts or examined by students in the field of marine biology.

Wave energy devices present the possibility to house new artificial reefs.

Footprints in the Sand

The most obvious and significant benefit of wave energy is that it is carbon-free. Wave energy offers the potential to power homes and cities with no harmful emissions. With the improvement of devices, the potential for wave energy to power homes on a commercial level is within sight. For example, the StingRAY can produce an average of 330 kW, or in other words, it can power approximately 330 homes. Imagine a wave farm of StingRAY devices. How many homes could a group of StingRAY devices power?

The current power output does not represent the possibilities within reach. For example, it has been mentioned that the StingRAY can produce up to 500 kW in stormy weather. Yet, with improvements it is expected to produce up to 600 kW.

CRITICAL THINKING

- What type of wave power–generating device do you think has the most significant benefits? What are these benefits?

- What are some positives of wave energy? What are some negatives?

- How would the commercialization of wave energy be a good thing?

The full impact wave energy devices have on local habitats and the many animals that call them home cannot be determined until devices are tested in groups.

Chapter 3

Disadvantages of Wave Power

As great as wave energy is, there are certain drawbacks to using this kind of energy. No single engineer, biologist, or researcher can get rid of all of wave energy's disadvantages. It can be difficult to determine what disadvantages wave energy presents today, and what problems it will face tomorrow. Wave energy is still growing, and ever changing. As much potential as wave energy has for good, there are clearly some important concerns. In order to form a clearer picture of wave energy's potential and impact, it is important to consider both present and future concerns about wave energy, whether they are proven yet or not.

Friend or Foe?

Marine biologists have voiced concerns for the habitats and wildlife that wave energy may influence. They are worried that wave energy devices may harm habitats and negatively affect wildlife. Because wave energy devices are generally tested individually rather than in a group, it can be difficult to predict how having many wave energy devices together in one area would affect local habitats. Until wave energy is more commercialized or wave farms are used at a larger scale, marine biologists cannot be sure what the impact will be on local habitats.

To understand the amount of time it takes to determine the impact of renewable sources of energy, let's consider wind energy. The effect of wind energy on birds has been studied for over ten years. Furthermore, unlike wave energy, wind energy is used on a larger, commercial scale. Even so, it is still difficult to determine the exact impact that windmills have on bird populations. Many more years of study will be needed before experts can assess the true environmental impact of new devices for wind and wave energy.

Wave energy is just breaking into use in the commercial market. It is uncertain whether or not wave energy will have a negative impact on wildlife. Time and research are needed to discover if potential negative impacts of wave energy will truly affect the surrounding environment. There is still a lot of uncertainty surrounding wave energy's environmental impact, and as the world moves toward safer and more environmentally focused energy resources, this is a drawback. The concern surrounding potential negative impacts can make it more difficult for projects to get started. As a result, this makes it difficult to discover what problems wave energy truly presents.

Wildlife Worries

Wave energy developers must consider the effect on underwater and above-water wildlife. One concern marine biologists have presented is the potential negative effect turbine sound may have on whales and other creatures that use sound to communicate. Because marine biologists and wave energy developers are only given the opportunity to monitor singular devices during their testing periods, they cannot determine the effect that multiple devices will have on wildlife. Due to cost and risk factors, devices are tested individually and often at a smaller scale. Because wave energy must have multiple devices in one area producing energy in order to provide a significant amount of electricity, the impact of the sound of multiple turbines in one area needs to be tested. Testing in this way will enable us to determine the ecological impact, if any, and protect local wildlife.

Wave farms would contain many devices consolidated, or grouped together, in one area. Therefore, until more wave energy devices are deployed, it will be difficult to discover whether or not turbine sound actually negatively affects whales. If turbine sound does affect whales, the displacement of whales and other creatures, possible damage to them, and potential disruption to their communication would be important negative effects to consider. Therefore, biologists will need to continue to monitor the area around devices as wave energy improves.

Another problem is that tests only span a limited period of time. The limited amount of time wave energy developers are given to test makes it difficult to understand how a device permanently deployed in water will affect the surrounding area. Think of wind energy. Remember that scientists still haven't decided the turbines' effect on birds. However, there is research that supports the idea that the installation of wave devices actually might cause the most harm to marine life. Loud sounds during the deployment might harm wildlife with sensitive hearing. The disruption in the water may have other negative effects. The decommissioning of devices, or the period of time when they are taken out of water, also presents these concerns.

The Data We Have

So far we have discussed possible but not yet confirmed disadvantages of wave power. In contrast, researchers have confirmed that exposed parts of

The wildlife below and above the surface needs to be monitored for possible impact when wave power devices are working nearby.

wave energy devices are a credible concern. Many researchers worry that marine wildlife might accidently run into devices. Currently, the damage is expected to be insignificant, but it is still something to consider. Another significant concern is that animals might get tangled in the cables used to transport electricity to shore. These cables often float freely in the water, which creates a risk to local wildlife. Additionally, electromagnetic fields that are produced by the cables could affect species sensitive to these fields—such as marine mammals, sharks, sawfish, rays, bony fish, skates, and sea turtles.

We have considered the effect turbines and cables may have on underwater animals, but what about local wildlife that lives above water? Like wind power, wave power may negatively affect birds. However, while wind turbines are a risk to birds, wave energy turbines are not. Because they are located underwater, the turbines pose no risk to sea birds. So how might wave energy affect sea birds? In some cases, floating or buoy devices may inhabit areas where sea ducks live. As a result, the buoys might cause sea ducks to relocate. It is important to consider wildlife below and above water when deploying wave energy devices.

With more time and research, the full impact of wave farms on animal habitats can be determined. Knowing how these farms change the environment around them will help us better protect all aspects of the environment. Wave energy does not emit carbon into the atmosphere, and it is a renewable energy. Both of these factors are outstanding advantages to our environment. However, we still need to consider other ways we might affect the environment when placing new technologies in new, previously untapped areas.

Costly Beginnings

Presently, the cost of wave energy is more than wind and coal. The Ocean Energy Council reports that the best wave energy technology in the United Kingdom produces energy at an average 7.5 cents per kWh. In comparison with wind, which is 4.5 cents per kWh, and coal, an average 2.6 cents per kWh, wave energy is much more expensive.

Not only is wave energy technology expensive, but also it has many hidden expenses. Because many devices are still in the testing stages, there are extra costs. These include extra equipment and staff to monitor devices' effects on wildlife and local ecosystems, as well as extra safety precautions to ensure the devices will not sink. If a device does sink, there are additional costs to retrieve the device to prevent it from harming local habitats. The cost for retrieving a device can be in the millions. For example, Finavera's device sank during its testing period in 2007. The AquaBuOY was only a $2 million device, but retrieving it was a multimillion-dollar project. Although costly, these extra amounts are an important consideration in the testing stages and are included in the early stage costs. Hopefully with improvement and commercialization these costs will decrease. Nonetheless, the costs can be a barrier to success and hurt wave energy companies attempting to grow and become more marketable.

Testing costs, such as the use of testing facilities, locations, boats, and staff to deploy the machines are a considerable challenge facing wave energy development. Tests aren't only done to gather data on the environment or to ensure that devices will float, however. Testing devices also allows developers to redesign, increase durability, and increase efficiency. Companies hope these extra costs are paid back when a breakthrough or increase in efficiency occurs. They are an important necessity. Funding or support can be difficult to obtain while wave energy developers search for the right design. In power, a sure success is always more appealing to people who might invest than a "maybe" device. When a device proves its durability, efficiency, and overall promise of

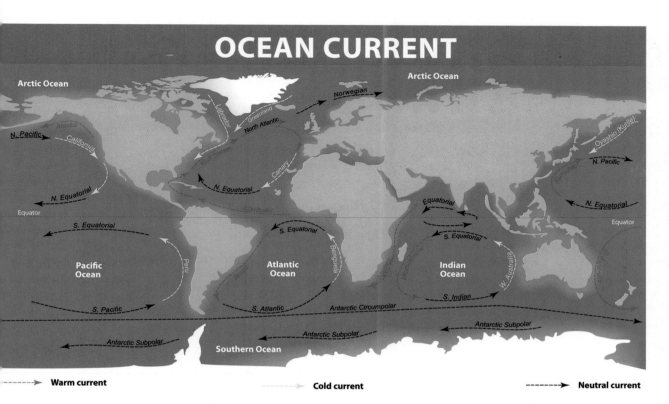

OCEAN CURRENT

Arctic Ocean

Arctic Ocean

Labrador

Greenland

Norwegian

Ovashio (Kurile)

N. Pacific

Alaska

California

North Atlantic

N. Pacific

N. Equatorial

Canary

N. Equatorial

N. Equatorial

Equator

Equator

S. Equatorial

S. Equatorial

Equatorial

S. Equatorial

Peru

Benguela

W. Australia

Pacific
Ocean

Atlantic
Ocean

Indian
Ocean

S. Indian

S. Pacific

S. Atlantic

Antarctic Circumpolar

Antarctic Subpolar

Antarctic Subpolar

Antarctic Subpolar

Antarctic Subpolar

Southern Ocean

------> Warm current

------> Cold current

------> Neutral current

Ocean currents are a vast power source hidden in the ocean that wave power generators cannot harness. Could scientists be studying the wrong alternative energy sources in our oceans?

profit, funding and investments are easy to secure. However, funding and testing is needed to get to this point. In some cases, developers need to find a company or investor willing to take a risk. However, no matter what improvements a company makes to a device, the cost of testing and redesigning, although necessary for future development of wave energy, can hinder or prevent wave energy's progress.

A DEEPER DIVE

Surf or Convert

Some surfing communities have expressed opposition to wave energy. Their main concern is that devices will be deployed in local surfing areas. There is the additional concern that wave energy technology might affect wave height because wave energy devices extract energy from the waves. However, there is no conclusive evidence that wave farms affect wave height. As we have observed in previous cases, future monitoring is necessary to determine if wave energy presents a credible disadvantage to surfing communities.

There was considerable concern around the deployment of the Wave Hub in the southwest region of the United Kingdom. Surfer opposition was covered in the media, making it clear that the issue of wave energy devices in surfing areas needed to be addressed. What was represented in the media was a much larger impact on wave height than had been predicted by some studies. This kind of misrepresentation or confusion of information can create

It is important to consider the impact wave energy has on local communities and recreation.

barriers for future wave energy development and causes wave energy developers to lose needed local support. This incident, among others, proves that it is important for wave energy companies to consider and communicate with local populations that may be affected by their products. Forming partnerships, gathering data, and presenting accurate information may prevent potential setbacks. It's important to consider the people involved as well as the wildlife.

Finding a Wave

Although the ocean covers 71 percent of the Earth, finding a place for wave energy farms is still a challenge. Coastal areas—the ideal spot for wave farms—are already used for tourism, fishing, surfing, shipping, and living. Many other coastal areas are protected or used for oceanographic research. Suddenly the area for harnessing wave power becomes much smaller. Because wave energy is so new, it is not currently a part of the territorial sea plan.

Wave devices are most efficient in conditions with consistent wind and strong, regular waves. These factors further limit areas available for use. Areas such as the western coasts of the United States and Australia, the southern coast of Africa, and the coasts of northern Canada and Scotland provide ideal conditions. However, the presence of coastal recreational use and other already established industries limits the use of these areas.

Offshore sites and reclusive areas provide a place for wave farms if they don't interfere with protected ocean habitats. These sites have their disadvantages, though. Remember that wave farms need to be somewhat close to the shore. For instance, wave energy technology is less advanced in offshore sites, and the farther away from the coast, the more cost is added for long cables to transfer energy to shore.

Stormy Weather

Probably the biggest challenge to wave energy is in its title: waves. The risk of damage to these expensive devices is a top concern for wave energy developers. In fact, the main goal of testing is to provide solutions

However rare, monster waves could destroy future wave energy farms. Devices must be prepared for conditions much worse than they will usually see while in the ocean.

to this threat. Ocean storms can create larger-than-average waves—waves that the devices will come in contact with less often. For example, the average wave that hits the coast of Oregon is 47 feet (14 m) tall, but waves have reached a height of 95 feet (29 m). Wave energy devices need to be designed so they can harness wave power for electricity in both modest and extreme conditions. More importantly, they need to not be destroyed when encountering extreme conditions. It is difficult for wave energy developers to predict and design devices for such conditions. Nonetheless, devices *are* being designed and tested with these risks in mind. Columbia Power's StingRAY is one example. Perhaps there is a design yet to be discovered or just being discovered at this moment that will solve this problem.

Trial and Error

It seems wave energy's questions are its biggest disadvantage and will shift with our growing knowledge and experience with this renewable energy. Perhaps there are unknown negative outcomes yet to be discovered. Perhaps there are solutions, too. The necessary trial and error process will unveil problems, giving wave energy enthusiasts the opportunity to fix them.

CRITICAL THINKING

- Researchers debate whether or not monitoring the impacts on marine wildlife is worth the cost. Some argue that this cost slows down the development of wave energy and its positive impact on our environment, while others argue it is necessary to monitor all of wave energy's projected impacts. Where do you stand?

- Hiccups such as the sinking of AquaBuOY can be viewed as opportunities for improvement or barriers to success. What do you think and why?

- What other potential obstacles do you think wave energy might face in its future?

Coasts, an ideal spot for wave farms, are used for other purposes, like fishing and other aquatic recreation. Wave energy developers work to predict the actual ocean area available for development.

Chapter 4

What's Happening in Our Waters?

According to a study by the Electric Power Research Institute (EPRI), the waters surrounding the United States contain 2,640 **terawatt-hours per year** (TWh/yr) of potential wave energy. The unit TWh/yr simply means how many terawatts per hour can be produced annually. There are 1,000,000,000 kilowatts in each individual terawatt. That's a lot of electricity! Recent discussion about how other industries, like fishing or tourism, interfere with wave energy suggests that looking at the total amount of ocean energy available is not practical. The EPRI conducted an analysis of the US coastal ocean resource that measured the **recoverable resource** of the sea, or the energy actually available to us. In 2011, it concluded that there are a total of 1,170 terawatt-hours per year of potential energy available to harness. This is about one-third of the total amount of electricity the United States consumes yearly.

So what does this mean for wave energy? This figure only represents the recoverable resource on the US coasts. There are a lot more terawatts of potential energy out there to tap into in other countries. The future of wave energy relies on the resources of money and technological

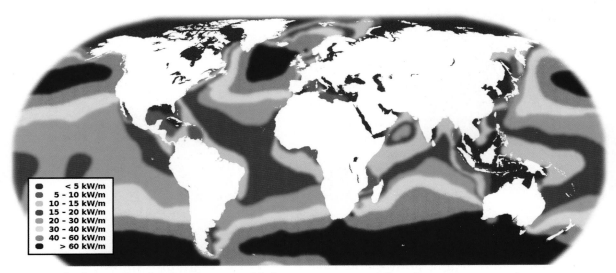

●	< 5 kW/m
●	5 – 10 kW/m
●	10 – 15 kW/m
●	15 – 20 kW/m
●	20 – 30 kW/m
●	30 – 40 kW/m
●	40 – 60 kW/m
●	> 60 kW/m

The better the design, the more likely wave energy will make its way onto the ocean map—literally and figuratively.

advancements. Even more so, it relies on invested people willing to take risks. Companies need to be willing to lose money in order to gain.

With the projected rise of natural gas prices, the push to fund other resources could benefit wave energy. Some companies, like Ocean Power Technologies, have focused on improving technology before launching devices in the water, which they hope will benefit them when funding eventually increases for wave power.

What about Tidal Power?

Tidal power is one of the oldest forms of energy used. Tides are another way water moves through the ocean. If you've ever spent a day by a big body of water or on a coast, you may have noticed that at different points during the day the water increases and recedes along the shoreline.

Undersea tidal power utilizes the power of the tides to spin underwater turbines. Much like wave power, the market for undersea tidal power is still under development. Unlike wave power, however, tidal power is entirely predictable due to the regularity of tidal patterns. Whereas wave power is more predictable than wind, tidal power is the most predictable of the three energy sources. There are three main methodologies for tidal energy today, but only one that uses the power of ocean tides without needing an enclosed area. This approach is called **tidal stream** turbines. Tidal stream turbines are a unique approach to capturing coastal ocean energy. They use tidal streams, or the currents created by the rise and fall of the tides.

In order to fully understand tidal energy and what it looks like, let's take a look at one of the innovative designs being used today. Understanding tidal energy will help explain how it differs from wave energy and how both of these marine energy markets are growing alongside one another. Tidal energy turbines look a lot like wind turbines except that they are located underwater. On May 20, 2015, Wales launched an underwater kite turbine project that will generate thirty new jobs and power up to eight thousand homes. This quick success stemmed from the first development of underwater kites in 2009. The concept was originally designed for wind, but then was determined to be better suited for the water. Twenty underwater kites are involved in the project, forming a **tidal stream farm**. The kites are tethered by a cable to the seafloor about 50 feet (15 m) below the water's surface. Each kite has a turbine that spins as the kite moves in a figure eight shape in the tidal streams. Off the coast of Anglesey in waters called Holyhead Deep, the project provides new jobs, renewable energy, and grounds for future growth.

Underwater kites, such as this one, are being used to generate electricity in places such as Colombia and Zambia.

On December 22, 2014, Scotland announced the groundbreaking of the world's largest tidal farm. The project involves the deployment of 269 tidal turbines. Each turbine can produce 1.5 **megawatts (MW)** of electricity, a whopping amount. One megawatt is equal to 1,000 kilowatts. The project will power about 175,000 homes in the United Kingdom when fully implemented, and 60 of the 269 total turbines will be installed and producing power by 2020. The project is part of Scotland's goal to generate 100 percent of its electricity demand from renewable energy by 2020.

Tidal units rest below the surface and extract energy from the consistent day-to-day tides.

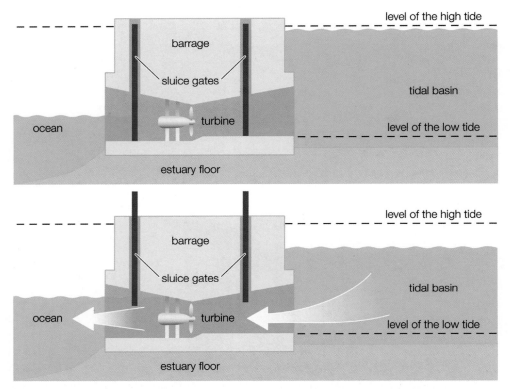

level of the high tide

barrage

sluice gates

tidal basin

turbine

ocean

level of the low tide

estuary floor

level of the high tide

barrage

sluice gates

tidal basin

ocean

turbine

level of the low tide

estuary floor

Tidal energy is designed so the blades move slowly, lessening the chance for collision with wildlife. This kind of tidal barrage is often used in bays and rivers.

Tidal energy's market is slowly growing alongside wave energy. They share many of the same advantages: they are both emission free, have little visibility (in tidal energy's case, no visibility), and are highly predictable and consistent. They share disadvantages too: concerns for wildlife, current cost, and finding a way to work with other industries that are territorial of the seacoast. However, tidal energy brings unique solutions as well as problems to the marine energy market.

Tidal energy shows inconclusive results regarding its impact on wildlife because of its small market lifespan. **Tidal fences**, or rows of linked tidal turbines, are the biggest concern today. Tidal fences can actually alter the natural tidal range. Changes could reduce feeding sites for birds or impact salt marshes. They could also reduce the transfer of sediment to the shoreline, which could affect shoreline erosion.

Although there are concerns about the effect of tidal turbines on the tides, they are designed with precautions. Tidal turbines are designed so the energy extracted from the tide is small yet efficient, so they do not significantly affect the tides. Additionally, the blades of the turbine move slowly, so the risk of collision with marine wildlife is small. If there is a collision, it is unlikely to cause significant damage. Screens can even be placed on tidal turbines to further protect wildlife from them.

The biggest benefit of tidal energy is that it is entirely predictable. The predictability of the tides reduces project risk because it allows companies to design tidal turbines with these patterns in mind, optimizing their efficiency. Although waves are quite reliable, tides are on a daily schedule, making it easier for developers to design machines that will respond to these patterns. Another advantage of marine tidal energy is that there is no visibility. Like M3's DMP device, tidal turbines solve the problem of visibility to coastal communities—a problem that can make it so difficult for ocean energy technology to find its way on the territorial sea plan—because they are always submerged in water. As wave energy and tidal farms are improved and implemented, it will be interesting to see which technology succeeds and grows its market share.

Marine Energy in the Present

We've covered how kinetic energy is extracted from our waters, what kinds of marine energy devices are present, and what projects have occurred, but what is happening in our waters today? Every month new projects, partnerships, and advances are announced. Let's take a look at some new advances in the field. Wave energy has a big future. It's at the cusp of gathering speed. Hopefully its future is as vast as the oceans that it harnesses.

Partnerships can take many forms and are vital for wave energy. In 2008, the Scottish government announced the Saltire Prize, a £10 million prize for the marine energy design that generates at least 100 **gigawatt-hours (GWh)** of electricity over a two-year period. Although the money offered doesn't cover the costs it takes for wave energy companies to deploy and maintain their machines, it does provide publicity, a forum to compete and share ideas, networking, and the opportunity and location for testing. Opportunities like these are needed and a contest is a great way to gather unique ideas and efforts toward wave energy.

As of 2015, four energy companies have entered the competition. The projects they are working on are DP Marine Energy's West Islay tidal project, Aquamarine Power's Oyster 800, MeyGen's tidal energy scheme, and ScottishPower Renewables' tidal turbines. The prize, once awarded, will also bring attention to wave energy that can only help the market grow. Naturally, the most attention will be given to the company that holds the winning model. The other companies involved, however, will also benefit from the visibility the competition offers.

Contests provide a unique opportunity to test devices and share ideas.

Although submitting a wave energy device to a contest may not promise immediate profit, the publicity often provides future opportunity for funding and public education about wave energy developments.

Although the money awarded is not a great amount, the contest allows companies to test for free. The challenge to consistently provide energy gives the companies involved an opportunity to test their technologies' true output and improve it as well. Testing facilities usually charge a high price or at least a minimal monthly fee. Contests, however, provide the testing location for the companies. Contests of this kind offer needed funding and locations for more extensive testing or testing for longer periods of time. The goal of the project, too, promises that the companies will have a solid idea of their marine energies' electricity output to advertise once the competition comes to a close. No matter who

A DEEPER DIVE

Grid Connection

As of July 2015, the United States deployed a device that connects to the Hawaiian grid. Northwest Energy Innovations' (NWEI) device, Azura, now provides 20 kW of no-emission electricity to the grid. And the device is only a half-scale prototype! The full-scale device can generate between 500 and 1,000 kW and will be deployed late in 2017 after a period of testing. Connecting devices to the grid allows them to provide renewable energy even in their testing phases, giving them credibility as they develop.

wins, each company will have gathered important information that is vital for improvement.

Another way wave energy technologies gain support is through government funding. As of October 2015, Wave Energy Scotland (WES), a state-funded organization committed to providing funding for innovative wave technologies, put out its second call for projects. The funding WES provides gives untested ideas and new companies the opportunity to advance wave energy technology. WES also allows some improved, previously tested designs to participate if they show promise. In other words, WES is making sure new companies can get their feet in the door. Contests and government organizations that solicit work give wave energy developers opportunities they might not otherwise have.

In the United States, the navy funds similar projects in Hawaii and off the western coast. As of April 2014, the US Navy partnered with the US Department of Energy to test three wave energy devices at Hawaii's energy test site. In October, they announced $10 million of funding for two companies to allow them to test devices in California and Oregon. Government partnering and funding provides the financial floor for future advances in renewable energies.

Chile Searches New Waters

In 2015, Chile partnered with a naval defense and marine energy organization in France called DCSN to build a marine energy research and development center in South America. The aim of the center is to work with Chilean educational organizations and companies to identify coastal sites in South America where marine energy devices could be installed. Chile has excellent conditions for waves, and this partnership will allow Chilean institutions and people to benefit from wave energy. Additionally, the installation of wave energy farms will also allow students, educators, and researchers to study wave energy. Global partnerships like these not only give opportunities for new jobs but also for education along with wave energy advancement. They make information available to new people and areas.

Sharing Secrets

An unexplored barrier to wave energy success is the nature of a competitive market. If companies do not share advances, then the same companies might make the same mistakes over and over again. Or, perhaps one company has found a solution to another company's problem, and vice versa. Trade secrets are often protected, so how can wave energy truly advance if these secrets aren't shared? The partnership between Scotland's Aquamarine Power and Wave Energy Scotland provides an excellent example of two organizations breaking this barrier. These organizations formed a contract to share advances, mainly regarding what Aquamarine learned from progress with its Oyster device. Wave energy is a fairly new industry, and with the multitude of designs trying to make their way on the market, it can be difficult to gather needed information for improvement. Sharing advancements and solutions to problems is needed. The goal, ultimately, is to reduce our detrimental emissions, and wave energy is a solution. These organizations provide an excellent example of ways to enhance wave energy research on a scale that is larger than the individual company and profit.

What Our Oceans Promise

It will only be so long before wave energy and other marine sources such as tidal move past the preliminary testing phases. The US Department of Energy projects that marine power sources—including wave, tidal, and hydroelectric power sources—can potentially provide 15 percent of the nation's electricity by 2030. Perhaps wave power will soon be competitive with other renewable resources and traditional power sources. Within the next few years to a decade, we may be hearing bigger news regarding wave energies.

CRITICAL THINKING

- What do you think will happen with renewable marine energy in the upcoming years?

- Do you think tidal or wave energy will succeed in the energy market?

Glossary

carbon emissions The harmful substances, especially carbon dioxide, that enter the atmosphere from sources such as the fuels used by airplanes, cars, trains, and buses.

drive shaft A rotating shaft that transmits power.

generator A device that transforms mechanical energy to electrical energy.

gigawatt-hour (GWh) A unit of electrical energy that equals the average power consumption of 1 billion watts or 1 million kilowatts per hour within a given time period.

high-pressure system A swirling mass of cool air that creates fair weather.

hydraulic ram An automatic pump in which a large volume of water flows through a valve that is periodically forced shut.

instantaneous power Power being consumed at this given moment.

kilowatt (kW) A unit of power.

kilowatt-hour (kWh) A measure of electrical energy that equals the average power consumption of 1,000 watts or 1 kilowatt per 1 hour within a given time period.

low-pressure system A swirling mass of warm, moist air that brings about good, strong waves and/or stormy weather.

megawatt (MW) A unit of electrical power that equals 1,000 kilowatts or 1 million watts.

national grid A network of high-voltage power lines connecting major power stations.

recoverable resource The amount of energy in the sea that is actually able to be harnessed for use.

terawatt-hours per year (TWh/yr) How many terawatt hours that can be produced annually. A terawatt is 1 billion kilowatts.

tidal fences Rows of linked tidal turbines.

tidal stream A current created by the rise and fall of the tides.

tidal stream farm An area where multiple tidal turbines are located.

tidal turbine Submerged turbine that is anchored to the ocean floor, bearing resemblance to a wind turbine.

velocity Speed of motion.

watt (W) A small unit of power, equivalent to 1 joule per second; there are 1,000 watts in every kilowatt.

wave farms A series of wave energy devices in one area producing electricity.

Find Out More

Books

Owen, Ruth. *Energy from Oceans and Moving Water: Hydroelectric, Wave, and Tidal Power.* Power: Yesterday, Today, Tomorrow. New York: PowerKids Press, 2013.

Peppas, Lynn. *Ocean, Tidal, and Wave Energy: Power from the Sea.* Energy Revolution. New York: Crabtree, 2008.

Rusch, Elizabeth. *The Next Wave: The Quest to Harness the Power of the Oceans.* Scientists in the Field. New York: Houghton Mifflin Harcourt, 2013.

Websites

Ocean Energy Council

www.oceanenergycouncil.com

The Ocean Energy Council site provides brief pros and cons about wave and tidal energy.

Tidal Energy Today

tidalenergytoday.com/category/news-by-topic/environment

Tidal Energy Today broadcasts brief stories about new wave and tidal energy projects.

Water Power Program

energy.gov/eere/water/water-power-program

The Office of Energy Efficiency and Renewable Energy (EERE) reports on new advancements of wave energy and provides wave energy facts.

Video

Energy 101: Marine and Hydrokinetic Energy

energy.gov/eere/videos/energy-101-marine-and-hydrokinetic-energy

The US Department of Energy explains different marine energy renewables and how they work.

Index

Page numbers in **boldface** are illustrations. Entries in **boldface** are glossary terms.

About the Author

Hannah Benning is a certified ESL instructor and library services specialist. As an educator and advocate for renewable energies, she practices contextualizing appropriate grade-level academic vocabulary in meaningful contexts within her writing and teaching.